Wise El on Life

30 More Cartoon Tips To Guide You Through Life

by

Euphrosene Labon

Wise El on Life

Other titles from the same author

Profit From Unlimited Thinking

A Little Book of Big Sales Tips

A Little Book of Self-Publishing Tips

A Little Book of Self-Coaching Tips

A Little Book of Time Tips

A Little Book of Abundance Tips

Wise El on Surviving Recessions Depressions And Downturns

This book will be available to order as a print book from all good bookshops. It may also be ordered directly from the publisher.

Additionally, it is available at quantity discounts for bulk purchase for business, educational or sales promotional use.

Please email euphrosene@euphrosenelabon.com for more information.

For my father, Louis, and Kamala Germaine, my mother.

First published in Great Britain in 2012 by
Floreo Publishing
Brambletyne Close
Angmering
West Sussex
BN16 4DD

ISBN 9781905402250

GENERAL/ NON-FICTION/ SELF-HELP/ PERSONAL DEVELOPMENT/ CARTOONS

Text © Euphrosene Labon

Cartoons © Euphrosene Labon

A catalogue record of this book is available from the British Library.

Design and word processing Floreo Publishing

Additional distribution www.euphrosenelabon.com

Email euphrosene@euphrosenelabon.com

#1 There's a fine line between disaster and reaching your destination

#2 keep your distance from an obstacle and it will be easier to see what is ahead

#3 Life is not
meant to be
a
popularity contest

#4 Live for today.
You never know
what's just around
the corner.

#5 Rejection
can be a
good motivator

#6 Wisdom
is knowing
when to
retreat

#7 When you are at life's crossroads, weigh up your options but always take action

#8 Trust sometimes means
taking a step
into the unknown

#9 Stand up
and
be counted

#10 Keep yourself clean and get great ideas too!

#11 Take time
to
take time

#12 Time will move faster
if you don't keep
a constant watch

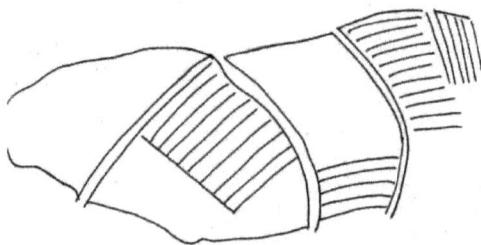

#13 Let your imagination
            drift
          from
      time to time

#14 A guru is someone we turn to
because
we do not trust
ourselves enough

#15 There is always
light
at some point

#16 Smile

#17 Failure
is a stepping stone
to
success

#18 Hugging
is good
for the soul

#19 The grass isn't always greener. Sometimes it's necessary to accept one's lot... for a while

#20 Desires need focus.
Having too many
can be an extra challenge
keeping them all
up in the air

#21 Try to take life lightly

#22 Grab opportunities
whenever they arise

#23 A weed is just a plant
with a strong survival instinct
growing in
the wrong place

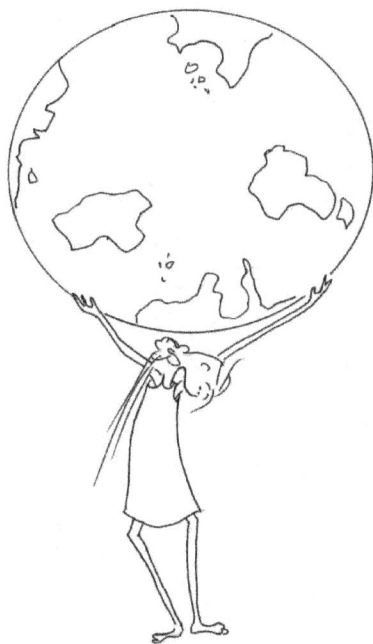

#24 carry the world on
your shoulders
and you'll be the only
one with the ache

#25 creativity
is its
own reward

#26 curiosity
keeps you
young

#27 Enjoy the scenery,
especially if the journey
requires effort

#28 Faith moves mountains –
in ways that work with
our logical minds

#29 Have big dreams

#30 If you could bottle
that energy,
imagine what you
could do with it,
thought Mason

LIFE QUOTATIONS

When I stand before God at the end of my life, I would hope that I would not have a single bit of talent left, and could say, 'I used everything you gave me'. **Erma Bombeck**

Believe that life is worth living and your belief will help create the fact. **William James**

Life consists not in holding good cards but in playing those you hold well. **Josh Billings**

While there's life, there's hope. **Marcus Tullius Cicero**

To live is the rarest thing in the world. Most people exist, that is all. **Oscar Wilde**

...to know that even one life has breathed easier because you have lived. This is to have succeeded. **Ralph Waldo Emerson**

Reality continues to ruin my life. **Bill Watterson**

All life is an experiment. The more experiments you make the better. **Ralph Waldo Emerson**

Any idiot can face a crisis - it's day to day living that wears you out. **Anton Chekhov**

A life spent making mistakes is not only more honorable, but more useful than a life spent doing nothing. **George Bernard Shaw**

The world you desire can be won. It exists.. it is real.. it is possible.. it's yours. **Ayn Rand**

Life can only be understood backwards; but it must be lived forwards. **Søren Kierkegaard**

Do not dwell in the past, do not dream of the future, concentrate the mind on the present moment. **Buddha**

Life is never easy for those who dream. **Robert James Waller**

The shoe that fits one person pinches another; there is no recipe for living that suits all cases. **Carl Jung**

We can never judge the lives of others, because each person knows only their own pain and renunciation. It's one thing to feel that you are on the right path, but it's another to think that yours is the only path. **Paulo Coelho**

He who has a why to live for can bear almost any how. **Friedrich Nietzsche**

We cannot change the cards we are dealt, just how we play the hand. **Randy Pausch**

We are taught you must blame your father, your sisters, your brothers, the school, the teachers - but never blame yourself. It's never your fault. But it's always your fault, because if you wanted to change you're the one who has got to change. **Katharine Hepburn**

Who says life is fair, where is that written? **William Goldman**

One lives in the hope of becoming a memory. **Antonio Porchia**

The purpose of life is to live it, to taste experience to the utmost, to reach out eagerly and without fear for newer and richer experience. **Eleanor Roosevelt**

Most men lead lives of quiet desperation and go to the grave with the song still in them. **Henry David Thoreau**

Life is nothing without a little chaos to make it interesting. **Amelia Atwater-Rhodes**

Life is an opportunity, benefit from it.
Life is beauty, admire it.
Life is a dream, realize it.
Life is a challenge, meet it.
Life is a duty, complete it.
Life is a game, play it.
Life is a promise, fulfill it.
Life is sorrow, overcome it.
Life is a song, sing it.
Life is a struggle, accept it.

Life is a tragedy, confront it.
Life is an adventure, dare it.
Life is luck, make it.
Life is too precious, do not destroy it.
Life is life, fight for it. **Mother Teresa**

There are two tragedies in life. One is to lose your heart's desire. The other is to gain it. **George Bernard Shaw**

Many people die at twenty five and aren't buried until they are seventy five. **Benjamin Franklin**

No man should ever completely realize his dreams. What else would there then be to live for? **David Gemmell**

At what age did I start to think that where I was going was more important than where I already was? When was it that I began to believe that the most important thing about what I was doing was getting it over with? **Colin Beavan**

You've got to get to the stage in life where going for it is more important than winning or losing. **Arthur Ashe**

It is never too late to be what you might have been. **George Eliot**

My life is my message. **Gandhi**

The three grand essentials to happiness in this life are something to do, something to love and something to hope for. **Addison**

We need not only a purpose in life to give meaning to our existence but also something to give meaning to our suffering. **Eric Hoffer**

Everyone is a house with four rooms, a physical, a mental, an emotional and a spiritual. Most of us tend to live in one room most of the time, but unless we go into every room, every day, even if only to keep it aired, we are not a complete person. **Indian Proverb**

SUGGESTED READING

How To Win Friends and Influence People –**Dale Carnegie**

Man's Search For Meaning –**Viktor Frankl**

The Life You Were Born To Live – **Dan Millman**

Golden Rules For Everyday Life – **Omraam Mikhaël Aïvanhov**

Living with Joy – **Sanaya Roman**

There Is A Spiritual Solution To Every Problem – **Wayne Dyer**

Discovering Your Soul's Purpose – **Mark Thurston**

Think Yourself To Health, Wealth & Happiness – **Joseph Murphy**

BRIEF BIOG

Euphrosene Labon is an artist, writer and author whose enthusiasm for learning and sharing her experience has also made her create a small publishing house. Make that a very small publishing house.

Her earlier career was predominantly in IT, as a successful sales and business development executive. Prior to that, she spent many years in training at Rank Xerox.

Euphrosene's main aim with her writings is to share the knowledge she has gained – and, hopefully, to make it easier for others to pursue and achieve their goals.

As well as the Little Book series, she has written **Profit From Unlimited Thinking** – a unique blend of timeless spiritual wisdom and business sense – to help the reader transcend any limitations in easy-to-follow steps.

She shares her spiritual journey, warts and all, through Delusions of Divinity?, her blog.

To read more, please visit
http://www.euphroselabon.com/modules/wordpress/

Life can be challenging and confusing.
This collection provides some easy
to follow rules to guide us on our way.

Wise El on Life is the latest in a series of
cartoon books designed to make
life and learning easier.

Floreo 33 Art And Books

www.euphroselabon.com

9781905402243